Super SCIENCE PROJECTS

You Can Make and Share

by Mari Bolte

illustrated by Paula Franco

CAPSTONE YOUNG READERS

a capstone imprint

Table of CONTENTS

Pack your bags for fun with the Sleepover Girls!
Every Friday, Maren, Ashley, Delaney, and Willow get
together for crafts, fashion, cooking, and, of course,
girl talk! Read the books, get to know the girls,
and dive in to this book of cool projects that are
Sleepover Girl staples!

Build an indoor ecosystem, or grow your own
geode jewels. Go green with bubble wrap earrings
and plant a gazing ball that goes with any garden.
Grab some glue, phone some friends, and start
crafting with your very own Sleepover Girls.

MEET THE SLEEPOVER GIRLS!

Willow Marie Keys

Patient and kind, Willow is a wonderful confidante and friend. (Just ask her twin, Winston!) She is also a budding artist with creativity for miles. Willow's Bohemian style suits her flower child within.

Maren Melissa Taylor

Maren is what you'd call "personality-plus"—sassy, bursting with energy, and always ready with a sharp one-liner. You'll often catch Maren wearing a hoodie over a sports tee and jeans. An only child, Maren has adopted her friends as sisters.

Ashley Francesca Maggio

Ashley is the baby of a lively Italian family. This fashionista-turned-blogger is on top of every style trend via her blog, Magstar. Vivacious and mischievous, Ashley is rarely sighted without her beloved "purse puppy," Coco.

Delaney Ann Brand

Delaney's smart, motivated, and always on the go! You'll usually spot low-maintenance Delaney in a ponytail and jeans (and don't forget her special charm bracelet, with charms to symbolize her Sleepover Girl buddies.)

Pine Cone *Fire Starters*

Whether the girls are camping outdoors or slumbering inside, the Sleepover Girls love bonfires! S'mores, anyone?

WHAT YOU'LL NEED

muffin tin and cupcake liners
tea lights, metal sleeves removed
pinecones
glitter
tweezers

1 Line a muffin tin with cupcake liners. Sprinkle glitter at the bottom of each liner. Then add a tea light.

2 Place muffin tin in a 300-degree Fahrenheit (150-degree Celsius) oven. With an adult's help, remove from the oven when the candles are completely melted.

3 Use tweezers to move the candle wicks to the edge of the cupcake liner.

4 Place a pinecone into each cupcake liner. Let the wax cool completely.

5 To use, place a pinecone at the base of your fire. Have an adult light the wick. The wick will ignite the pinecone and help start your fire.

SLEEPOVER SCIENCE

The candle wax will ensure the pinecone burns long enough to start the rest of your kindling on fire. You can easily change the color of the flame the pinecone produces by replacing the glitter with a simple household mineral. Only use one mineral at a time, and always have an adult for supervision.

YELLOW: table salt (sodium chloride)

YELLOW-GREEN: borax (sodium borate)

VIOLET: salt substitute (potassium chloride)

RED: boric acid powder (hydrogen borate)

WHITE: Epsom salts (magnesium sulfate)

Ombre Scarf

Science and style blend together in perfect harmony with this fabulous ombre scarf. Watch out, world—Magstar's taking on the world of science next!

clothing dye

white cotton scarf or long cotton fabric panel

clothes hanger

1 Prepare the dye according to the instructions on the package.

2 Wet the scarf in water. Then fold the scarf in half and drape over a clothes hanger.

3 Dip the scarf in the dye at the point where you want the lightest color to start. After a few seconds, pull the scarf out until only the tips of the scarf are in the dye.

4 Leave the tips of the scarf in the dye for the full amount of time, as directed by the package instructions.

5 Wash and dry according to package instructions.

SLEEPOVER SCIENCE

The dye moving up the fabric to create an ombre effect is called capillary action. The colored dye uses tiny gaps in the fabric's fiber to move. This is the same process plants use to bring water from the roots to the leaves.

Bacteri-Yum!

Can you handle the goo? Petri dishes filled with fruity gelatin make the perfect after-school treat for a science nerd like Delaney. Experiment with different colors and flavors of gelatin.

WHAT YOU'LL NEED

petri dishes

1 3-ounce (90-gram) box red gelatin

black food coloring

¼-ounce (7.5-gram) package of plain unflavored gelatin

2 tablespoons (30 milliliters) sour cream

sprinkles

Prepare red gelatin according to package directions.

 Divide red gelatin evenly among the petri dishes. Stir in a small amount of black food coloring to the dishes to vary the colors, if desired. Chill until set, about 1 hour.

 Place ¼ cup (60 mL) water in a microwave-safe bowl. Sprinkle unflavored gelatin on top and let stand 5 minutes. Then microwave for 30 seconds or until the gelatin dissolves. Stir in sour cream.

4 Pour gelatin mixture into two sandwich bags. Add black food coloring to one bag. Let cool about 15 minutes. Knead the bags every 5 minutes for even cooling.

5 Cut a small corner off the bags and pipe rows of curved lines and groups of small dots onto the petri dishes. Decorate other petri dishes with sprinkles.

SLEEPOVER SCIENCE

Petri dishes are used for growing cells, bacteria, and viruses. Scientists use a gelatinlike substance called agar, which is made from red algae. These edible petri dishes are much more appealing!

Sleepover Suckers

Not only do these lips make a funny prop for Maren's improv, they're tasty too!

WHAT YOU'LL NEED

lollipop mold

nonstick cooking spray

hard candy

lollipop sticks

sprinkles and small candies

1 Place lollipop mold on a baking sheet. Spray the mold with nonstick cooking spray. Then preheat oven to 300 degrees Fahrenheit (150 degrees Celsius.)

2 Place unwrapped candies in a zip-top bag. Crush with a hammer or rolling pin.

3 Pour crushed candy into lollipop mold. Pile the candy high; it will melt down.

4 Place baking sheet and lollipop mold in the oven. It should take about 5 minutes for the crushed candy to melt.

5 Carefully remove the baking sheet from the oven. Add lollipop sticks to the mold. Add more crushed candy to cover. Return the baking sheet to the oven for another 2-3 minutes.

6 Remove the baking sheet from the oven. Decorate lollipops with sprinkles and hard candies, if desired. Let the lollipops cool completely before removing from the mold.

TIP:
If your lollipops break when removing them from the mold, just re-crush and re-melt the candy. You can even reuse the stick!

SLEEPOVER SCIENCE

Hard candy is made with sugar heated to about 300 F. The sugar melts into a syrup. As it cooks, the water boils away and raises the syrup's temperature. The temperature tells you what the syrup will be like once it cools. For example, syrup heated to around 240 F (115 C) will be sticky and easy to stir, and is best used for things like marshmallows or gummies. Syrup at around 270 F (132 C) is firmer but still pliable, and used for taffy. Syrup heated to 320 F (160 C) becomes caramel.

Jewel-Toned *Geodes*

Turn home-grown geodes into your newest accessory. Make the mixure at one sleepover. After the crystals grow for a week or two, schedule a second sleepover to finish up the project.

WHAT YOU'LL NEED

1 cup (240 mL) water
two glass containers
2 heaping tablespoons (30 mL) alum
metal locket blank
decoupage glue
watercolor paints (optional)
clear nail polish

1 Heat water in a glass container until hot but not boiling. Stir in alum powder.

2 Set the container aside to let crystals grow. This could take one to two weeks.

3 When crystals are your desired size, carefully remove them from the bottom of the container. Let them dry completely before handling.

4 Paint the inside of the metal lock blank with decoupage glue.

5 Press pieces of crystal into the wet decoupage glue until the entire locket is covered. Let dry completely.

6 Use watercolor paint to color the crystals, if desired. Use as little water as possible to avoid washing away the decoupage glue.

SLEEPOVER SCIENCE

Alum is sold in the spice aisle at grocery stores. It is used as a water purifier and as a preservative. Crystals are formed through evaporation. The crystals grown in this project are called seed crystals. To make one large crystal, select the largest crystal in step 3. Then tie it to a string and suspend in a glass of alum in room temperature water. Let it grow until it's of the desired size.

7 Once the paint has dried, seal the entire locket with clear nail polish.

Easy Ecosystems

Willow keeps nature close at all times. This mini ecosystem, complete with arthropods or snails, is about as close as you can get!

WHAT YOU'LL NEED

glass container with airtight lid

pond scum

sand, stones, and shells

water plant

freshwater arthropods or snails

1 Rinse container with tap water, if necessary, but do not use soap. Set in a warm, sunny place until completely dry.

2 Add pond scum. It should be mostly liquid, with less than an inch (2.5 centimeters) of gravel or sand at the bottom of the jar. If your water is cloudy, add a little distilled water.

3 Add the plant.

4 Add the arthropods or snails.

5 Tightly seal the container. Your ecosystem should be set near light but not directly in sunlight.

SLEEPOVER SCIENCE

Visit a local pond, creek, or marshy area to find pond scum. Collect scum in a container. Be sure to include debris such as pebbles or mud. These will contain bacteria and microorganisms necessary to your ecosystem. If you are able to find a small water plant or a bit of moss there, use it. Otherwise check fish or gardening stores for cuttings. The plant will filter the water, produce oxygen, and feed the microorganisms in the ecosystem.

The arthropods and snails, known as scud, will keep your ecosystem clean as they eat decayed plant matter. Your pond scum may already come with scud attached. Otherwise pond snails or brine shrimp can be purchased along with your water plant.

Paparazzi Soap

Look your best for the paparazzi by washing with these fantabulous accessory-shaped soaps. Glitter makes them extra fun!

WHAT YOU'LL NEED

scissors or hole punch

tissue paper

glycerin soap block

soap molds

glitter

*

1   Use scissors or a hole punch to turn the tissue paper into small pieces of confetti.

2 Break glycerin into small pieces and place in a microwave-safe bowl. Microwave for 30 seconds. Stir, and microwave for another 30 seconds or until fully melted.

3 Fill soap mold halfway with glycerin.

4 Sprinkle confetti and glitter over the glycerin.

5 Add glycerin until mold is filled.

6 Sprinkle more confetti and glitter over the glycerin. Use a toothpick to gently stir in the confetti and glitter.

7 Let soap cool for at least half an hour, or until set.

SLEEPOVER SCIENCE

Glycerin is a natural by-product of the soapmaking process. It is a thick, colorless liquid known as a humectant—it naturally attracts and retains moisture. Compare its texture and appearance to a regular bar of soap.

Glycerin makes a gentle, soothing soap that keeps skin soft and smooth. It's mild enough for pets or babies and works well with any skin type.

Star Power

The Sleepover Girls can sleep under the stars even when they're indoors. Choose from dozens of constellations to create this sky-inspired artwork!

WHAT YOU'LL NEED

8 inch (20.3 cm) square stretched canvas

screwdriver

paint and paintbrush

silver glitter

hot glue and hot glue gun

battery-powered LED lights

1 Pick the constellation you want to use. Sketch the star pattern onto the canvas.

2 Use the screwdriver to carefully punch a small hole in the center of each star. For realism, make the holes different sizes, depending on the size of the stars in the constellation.

3 Paint the canvas. Loosely sprinkle glitter across the canvas while the paint is still wet. Let dry completely.

4 Flip the canvas over. Push a light through one of the holes. Secure with hot glue. Continue until there is a light in every hole.

5 Use hot glue to secure the battery pack to the canvas' wood frame.

SLEEPOVER SCIENCE

Constellations are groups of bright stars that appear near each other in the sky. People use constellations as a way to find and identify stars from Earth. There are 88 recognized constellations. The most famous and easy-to-see constellations include Orion, Ursa Major (the Big Dipper), Ursa Minor (the Little Dipper), and Casseopeia.

Sounds of the Sea

When Maren's mom's job takes the Taylors to the ocean, they love to collect sea glass on the shore. This windchime is the perfect way to let that glass shine.

WHAT YOU'LL NEED

jute rope

S hook

starfish shell

thin craft wire

sea glass

1 Attach one end of the rope to the S hook.

2 Tie the other end of the rope around the starfish. Wrap the rope several times around the body for security.

3 Wrap the craft wire around the sea glass to create a string of glass 6 or 7 pieces long. Leave a little space between the glass pieces.

4 Repeat until you have 10 strings of sea glass.

5 Attach the strings to the starfish. Tie five along the outer arms and five closer to the center.

SLEEPOVER SCIENCE

Sea glass is made from discarded bottles and other bits of glass in the ocean. The ocean's waves and currents tumble the glass, giving it a smooth surface. The chemicals used to make the glass are slowly removed, leaving small pits and sparkly mineral deposits on the glass' surface. It takes about 10 years for glass to become sea glass. Glass smoothed by lakes and rivers is called beach glass.

Bubble Wrap *Baubles*

Environmentalist Willow always follows the three Rs—reduce, reuse, and recycle. When she comes across a plastic bag that can no longer be reused, she recycles it. The result is remarkable!

WHAT YOU'LL NEED

toothpick

bubble wrap

plastic grocery bag

iron

parchment paper

¾-inch (2 centimeter) hole punch

small hole punch

jump rings

beads

earring wire

1 Use toothpick to prick each bubble from the bubble wrap.

2 Cut bubble wrap and grocery bag into strips 2 inches (5 cm) wide and 3 inches (7.6 cm) long. Sandwich one piece of grocery bag between two layers of bubble wrap. Then fold the layers between parchment paper.

3 Use an iron on the wool setting over the parchment paper for 30 seconds. Let plastic cool completely.

4 Add another piece of grocery bag over the cooled plastic. Then replace parchment paper and repeat step 2. Continue adding bubble wrap and grocery bag in alternating layers until you have at least 7 layers fused together.

5 Use the ¾-inch punch to cut out shapes from the fused plastic. Use the small hole punch to make a hole near the top edge of each shape.

6 Thread a bead onto a jump ring. Then thread a plastic piece onto the jump ring.

7 Attach the jump ring to an earring wire. Repeat so you have a pair of earrings.

SLEEPOVER SCIENCE

The first plastic grocery bags were introduced in the late 1970s. Plastic bags require less energy to create than paper bags. They also produce half the amount of greenhouse gases. Melting layers of plastic together fuses them into a durable waterproof fabric that can be cut out, sewn, or fused with more layers for thicker pieces of plastic.

Succulent Gazing Ball

Sweet garden balls make a charming addition to Maren's mom's wedding decor. They go perfectly with their succulent wedding favors.

WHAT YOU'LL NEED

small succulent plants with stems at least ¼-inch (0.6-cm) long

grapevine ball (available at craft stores)

sphagnum moss

spray bottle

ribbon

1 A few days before starting your project, trim the succulents into smaller sections, or cuttings. Leave the cuttings in a cool, dry area to allow the stems to dry out.

2 Stuff the grapevine ball with the moss. Lightly mist the ball and moss with water.

3 Tuck the succulent cuttings into one half of the grapevine ball. Tightly pack more moss around the succulent stems.

4 Set the ball aside, with the succulents facing up, for 5-6 days. This will allow the cuttings' roots to form.

5 Repeat step 3 with the other side of the grapevine ball. Tie ribbon to the top of the ball. Use ribbon to hang your garden with the newer cuttings at the top.

SLEEPOVER SCIENCE

Succulent plants hold on to moisture, allowing them to live in harsh, desertlike climates. They have shallow roots that grow back quickly. Popular succulents include cactus, aloe, and jade plants. Drying the stems before planting prevents the cuttings from absorbing too much water and rotting.

DIY Star Lights

These little spotlights let Ashley play around with different lighting and moods for her famous Magstar videos.

WHAT YOU'LL NEED

white paper

scrapbooking paper

spray adhesive

tin can

double-sided tape or craft glue

LED tea light

camera tripod

jewelry and metal glue

black tagboard

colored cellophane in various colors

tracing paper

*

1 Measure and cut a piece of white paper to fit around the inside the can. Use spray adhesive to attach the paper to the inside of the can.

Measure and cut a piece of scrapbook paper to fit around the outside of the can. Use spray adhesive to attach the paper to the outside of the can.

Use double-sided tape or craft glue to attach the tea light to the bottom of the can.

Attach the can to the tripod using jewelry and metal glue. Let dry completely.

*

5. To make color gels, cut a square of tagboard about 1 inch (2.5 cm) larger than your can. Trace the mouth of the can in the center of the cardboard square and cut out.

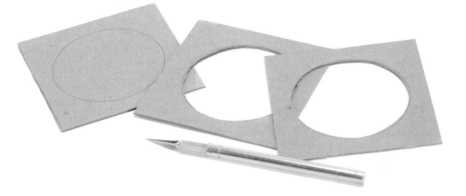

6. Cut pieces of cellophane and tracing paper the same size as your tagboard squares.

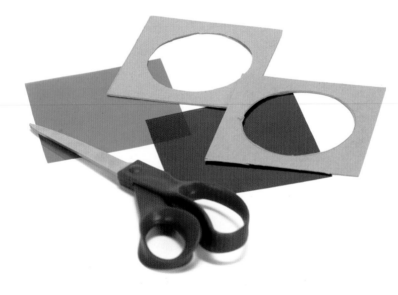

7 Sandwich a piece of cellophane between two pieces of tagboard. Staple together. Repeat with the rest of the cellophane and the tracing paper.

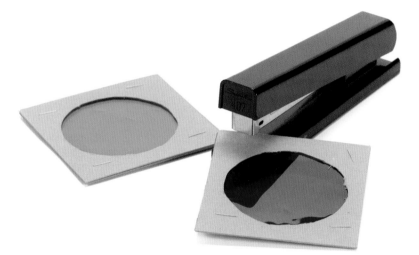

8 To use, turn on the LED tea light. Set a gel over the mouth of the can, if desired.

SLEEPOVER SCIENCE

Light reflects off the white paper inside the can, amplifying the light's brightness. The can concentrates the light into a narrower beam of light. The color gels allow light to pass through but change the way the light looks. They can deepen and intensify colors, or give your set a warmer or cooler look. Experiment with a variety of gels to get the right look. Or skip the gels—this also makes a great desk lamp.

Paper punch-outs bring
the Sleepover Girls to
life! From photo frames
and door hangers to
bookmarks and sticker
pages, you can bring
Maren, Delaney, Ashley,
and Willow wherever
you go.

insert photo

insert photo

USE PUNCH OUT FACES TO
ATTACH TO PARTY FAVORS ...

DECORATIONS, OR YOUR
OWN SLEEPOVER
INVITATIONS!

SHARE
OR DARE

shares

SHARE
OR DARE

dares

SHARE
OR DARE

shares

SHARE
OR DARE

dares

SHARE
OR DARE

shares

SHARE
OR DARE

dares

1. Hum the theme song to your favorite TV show. Keep humming until someone guesses it.

2. Put on makeup with your eyes closed. No cheating!

3. Change your ringtone to the most embarrassing song possible. No changing it back until someone calls you in public!

4. Show off your *American Idol* tryout skills.

---

1. What's the one item you wouldn't be caught dead with in public but can never throw out?

2. Who's your favorite male movie character?

3. If you needed rescuing, which superhero would you want to rescue you?

4. If you could change your ethnicity, age, or gender for the day, would you?

---

1. Draw a picture of your crush.

2. Call the last person you talked to or texted. Pretend you're ordering a pizza.

3. Decorate your face with sticky notes. Leave them there for three turns.

4. When someone talks to you, make sure your reply rhymes with whatever they just said.

---

1. Who's the last person you called or texted?

2. Tell me about the most amazing place you've ever been.

3. What's scarier—a giant shark or a giant dinosaur?

4. Have you ever done something you thought was right but later found out was wrong?

---

1. Wear the nearest item as a hat.

2. Have someone write your name on your forehead with a washable marker. For an extra dare, write it yourself—without looking in a mirror!

3. Take a selfie while making a funny face. Make it your profile picture.

4. Do your best celebrity impression.

---

1. What would you eat for your last meal?

2. Do you have a bad habit? What is it?

3. Name one thing you're great at. Then name one thing you wish you could do better.

4. What's your #1 pet peeve?

5. If you could date any famous celebrity, who would it be?

You're Invited

TO A SLEEPOVER!

With: _____

Where: _____

When: _____

RSVP: _____

With: _____

Where: _____

When: _____

RSVP: _____

USE THESE STICKERS TO CUSTOMIZE
FAVORS, DECORATIONS OR YOUR
SLEEPOVER INVITATIONS!

CRAFT IT
CIY
YOURSELF

sleepover Girls

Best
Friends

You're
Invited

Thank
You!

Sticker FUN!

KEEP THE PEACE

Earth to the Scientists!
What Kind of Scientist Are You?

There's so much more to science than creating cute crafts! The scientific world is just waiting for you to find your niche. This quick quiz will help you hypothesize which scientific field is the best match for you.

If you were a famous scientist, what would you want to be known for?

a) Discovering a new planet.
b) Curing a terminal disease.
c) Building the next generation of cars.

The tool you use the most is a:

a) multitool
b) microscope
c) calculator

Your favorite famous female scientist is:

a) Rachel Carson
b) Jane Goodall
c) Rosalind Franklin

Your favorite famous male scientist is:

a) Neil deGrasse Tyson
b) Jeff Corwin
c) Bill Nye

When you have spare time, you would rather:

a) take a nature hike or spend time outdoors looking at the stars.
b) volunteer at a nursing home or animal shelter.
c) do something with your hands, like working on a car or projects that involve building things.

The world is about to end! How do you think
it's going to happen?

a) A giant meteor is on its way to Earth. Duck and cover!
b) A zombie outbreak. Where's my zombie survival guide?
c) A supervillain has created a freeze ray to use
   on everyone.

Your favorite beauty products are:

a) mineral. I like to keep it natural.
b) organic. Being kind to the environment is important.
c) homemade. A little of this, a little of that, and voila!

How do you feel about global warming?

a) I don't like what it's doing to our planet.
b) Who is helping all the polar bears?
c) What can I do to help?

Your favorite TV show is:

a) *The Big Bang Theory*
b) *Grey's Anatomy*
c) *Dr. Who*

If you chose mostly "A" answers, you would rock as an **Earth and Space Scientist**! Understanding the world we live on is important to you, and you may find yourself dreaming of faraway places. You can't get much farther than outer space!

If you chose mostly "B" answers, your life's work is in **Life Science**! You're interested in life and relationships. That can mean studying the human body, the nerves and cells that make the body work, or even the places people live. "Get a life!" has a whole new meaning when you're around.

If you chose mostly "C" answers, you need to go hands-on with **Physical Science**! The world around you is fascinating. How was it made? How does it work? What else is out there? You and physical science have a chemistry that just can't be matched.

MAD LIB

The science fair was coming up and
Delaney needed a project. "What should I do
for an experiment?" she wondered. Willow was
testing if ＿＿＿＿＿＿＿＿＿ liked ＿＿＿＿＿＿＿＿ or
   _{type of rodent}   _{type of drink}
＿＿＿＿＿＿＿ better—using juice from her parents' smoothie place,
_{type of drink}
Creative Juices, obviously. Maren was paired up with Winston (of
course!) to see if ＿＿＿＿＿＿＿＿ liked being talked to by girls or boys
              _{type of plant}
better. Ashley was doing some kind of project involving ＿＿＿＿＿ and
                                             _{type of fabric}
＿＿＿＿＿＿ dye. "Everyone has a better idea than I do," Delaney sighed. Just
_{color}
then, Delaney's dog Frisco jumped onto the couch and ＿＿＿＿＿＿ her
                                          _{past-tense verb}
face. Delaney's sister Gigi always hated being licked in the face. "He's full
of germs," she complained. "That's it!" Delaney ＿＿＿＿＿＿＿ .
                                     _{past-tense verb}
"How germy are our mouths? That's a great project!
Thanks Frisco!" Frisco barked in reply. "Time to get started!"

sleepover Girls

Join the fun by following Delaney, Maren, Ashley, and Willow's adventures in the Sleepover Girls series!

Then start the party with Sleepover Girls Crafts. Each book will show you how to replicate the fashions, crafts, and recipes created by the Sleepover Girls.

FUN & FABULOUS CRAFT AND ACTIVITY TITLES

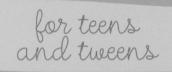

for teens and tweens

Capstone Young Readers are published by
Capstone, 1710 Roe Crest Drive, North Mankato,
Minnesota 56003.

www.capstoneyoungreaders.com

Library of Congress Cataloging-in-Publication Data
Bolte, Mari.
  Super science projects you can make and share /
By Mari Bolte.
      pages cm—(Sleepover Girls Crafts. Sleepover
girls crafts)
  Summary: "Step-by-step instructions, tips, and
full-color photographs will help teens and
tweens create science-based craft projects and
recipes"—Provided by publisher.
  ISBN 978-1-62370-422-3 (paperback)
1. Handicraft for girls—Juvenile literature. 2.
Science—Juvenile literature. I. Title.
  TT171.B65 2016
  745.50835—dc23
                                    2015023064

Designer: Tracy Davies McCabe
Craft Project Creators:
The Occasions Group
Creative Director: Nathan Gassman
Production Specialist: Laura Manthe

Photo Credits:
All photos by The Occasions Group
Photo Studio

Artistic Effects:
Shutterstock

Printed in China.
062015   009070RRDF15